From Tee to Green
for
Tot to Teen

From Tee to Green *for* Tot to Teen

A Parent's Guide to Getting Your Child Started in Golf

by

Teresa Kelly

Highview Press Inc.
2122 Highview Drive
Burlington, Ontario
Canada   L7R 3X4
www.highviewpress.com

ISBN 978-0-9680443-1-5

Printed and bound in Canada

Cover Design: Terry Syndergaard

Art: Terry Syndergaard

Cartoon Art

Chris Francis: pp. 13, 14, 20, 28, 37,40, 57, 61,
                 64, 69, 71, 75,81, 95, 107, 111

Michelle Junkin: pp. 27, 53, 101

This book is dedicated to
Sean Brendan John Kelly
— the next generation

Acknowledgments

As all authors know, books are never created by just one person. There are many people who contribute their knowledge, suggestions and opinions, and I would like to express my appreciation and gratitude to these people who offered their expertise in making this book possible.

Firstly, my gratitude goes to my family. My husband, Brendan Kelly, who is the greatest motivator, mentor and role model, who not only inspires, but offers his great publishing and computer skills and is my favorite golfing buddy, thank you for everything. My children, Aaron and Shannon, and daughter-in-law Melanie, who gave tirelessly in offering suggestions to improve the book, proofreading manuscripts and selecting appropriate art pieces – I couldn't have done it without you. To my little grandson, Sean who showed so much patience at such a young age to pose for photos and hit endless plastic golf balls in the park with his grandmother – you have enriched our family and our lives. To my sister, Hilda Cusson, who is always there for me, offering help whenever I need it and giving as unselfishly as possible, my complete appreciation.

To my artist, Terry Syndergaard whose enormous creative talents enhanced this project immensely. His sense of humor, patience, dedication and perfectionism contributed tremendously to the outcome of this book. My gratitude is also extended to Bonnie Erdrich, who assisted Terry with her computer enhancements. I am indebted to my longtime friend, Ron Sharp for introducing me to Terry. This project wouldn't have been the same without his input. Thanks also to my brother John Morris, who suggested I contact Ron Sharp. What goes around comes around!

To my colleague and friend, Robert Kraut and the staff at The Booklegger – Stan McKinzie, Libby Bonomolo, Sarah Hansen, Dallas Weinrich and Erica Glenn – who gave their time and effort in making suggestions to the manuscript to improve its quality, I am truly grateful.

To Hank Haney, who took precious time out of his busy schedule to offer his kind words in the Foreword of this book, I am indebted.

To Carrie Vaughan, who was Director of Golf Instruction at Hidden Lake Golf and Country Club at the time of this writing, this book would not be what it is without your expertise and input.

To the pro-shop staff at my home course of Hidden Lake Golf and Country Club in Burlington, ON, thank you for all the answers to the million questions I asked throughout the making of this book.

To the readers, friends and colleagues who offered suggestions, advice and encouragement – John Cormier, Kay Croft, Donna DiMarinis, Jodi Harrison, Gwen Myers, John Randle, Graham Shiels, Nancy Street – thanks for being there for me.

And finally to Yvonne Iken-Scott, my photographer who painstakingly took 250 photos in order for me to be able to select one half-decent picture of myself for this book, thank you for your patience and enormous talent.

About the Author

Teresa Kelly is a well-known children's author, having written many books such as *Acts of Courage*, *Famous Lives*, *Daring Deeds*, and *'Twas The Week Before Christmas*. Teresa was an editor and in-house author for a publishing company in Ontario, Canada, as well as a contributing editor for *Hamilton Cue* and *Hamilton This Month* magazines. She is now the president of the successful golf greeting card company *Golfing Lady*.

As a passionate, avid golfer, Teresa was interested in getting her two children started in golf. She successfully recruited her son, daughter and daughter-in-law to the lure of the links where they enjoy the game as competent, recreational golfers. She now is delighting in introducing the sport to her young grandson. Teresa lives with her husband Brendan in Burlington, Ontario, Canada during the summer months, and Naples, Florida in the winter months, enjoying golf 12 months of the year.

Foreword

As director of instruction for the International Junior Golf Academy in Hilton Head, South Carolina, I come in contact with parents every day. These parents, wanting the best for their children, inquire about the best possible way to get their children involved in golf. There is definitely a need in the market for a book that addresses all the questions parents are asking.

Teresa Kelly, well-known children's author, business-woman, parent and avid golfer also recognized that parents were looking for some direction in getting their kids started in golf. She met this need by authoring this book in a user-friendly, question-and-answer style that would be understood and appreciated by golfing and non-golfing parents alike. She addresses questions like: What age should my child start golf? What type of instruction should they have? Where can I locate a course with appropriate junior instruction? What equipment does a child need to get started? Included in this book is a wealth of information concerning schools, associations, Web site addresses and phone numbers, and children-friendly golf holidays.

This is a one-stop shopping guide that all parents should have to get their children started in golf. Whether to enhance a child's life with exposure to golf, or whether to prepare a child for a professional golfing career, the information in this book will provide the guidance that all caring parents are seeking.

Hank Haney

November, 2007

Introduction

As a parent I was interested in getting my two children involved in golf. Both my husband and I play golf, so it is only natural that we would want our children to play with us. It was so easy enrolling them in soccer, football, hockey, basketball, swimming, or dancing. The progression was natural in those activities – you simply enrolled your child in a sport or hobby that was either advertised in the local newspaper, or offered at school, and the kids advanced from there. Golf is more complicated.

Until recently, golf was considered a sport for old men who dressed in funny pants. Very few children were interested in playing golf. Adult men and women usually took up the sport after the kids left home and there was more time to spend on the golf course. No one had blazed a trail for parents who were interested in getting their young children started in golf. Thanks to a phenom named Tiger Woods, who blasted onto the golf stage at a very early age, golf has grown substantially in popularity. The game is experiencing a boom with more and more children discovering the joy of golf. That is why this book was created.

Many parents ask how they can get their children involved in golf without having them abandon the sport prematurely out of frustration. The search for information about starting children in golf can be as frustrating as the game itself! Though the Internet is an invaluable resource, tracking down answers to specific questions is an informational quagmire.

This little book is designed to guide you in making the best choices and answering all those questions you have about getting your child involved in golf. Your son or daughter will be the beneficiary of your efforts and will enjoy a lifetime of pleasure on the links.

Good luck!

Table of Contents

Chapter 1

Getting Started: Why, When and What Equipment?

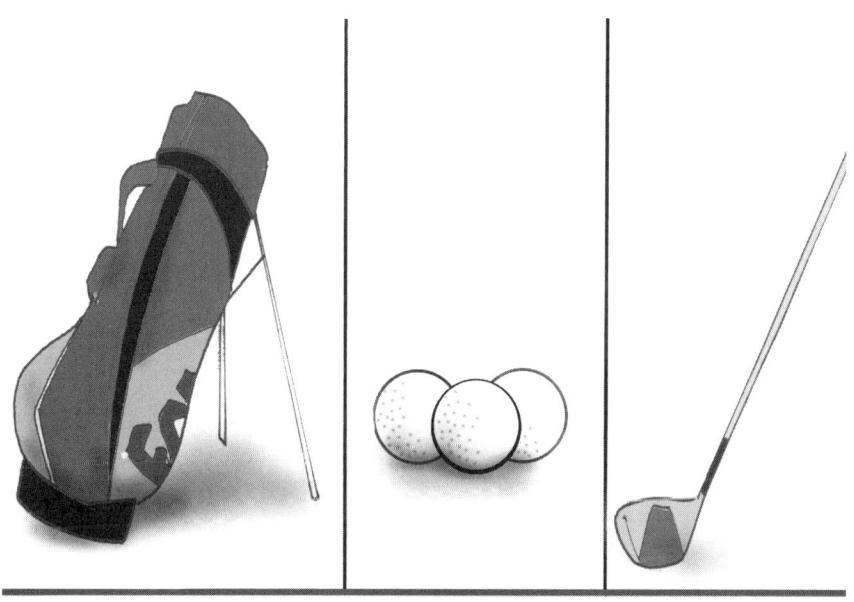

THE MOTIVATION: WHY SHOULD MY CHILD PLAY GOLF?

Although golf is a difficult sport to learn, there are several great reasons why you might like your child to play golf:

- You or your spouse plays golf and would like to continue the tradition by including your child.

- Your child has expressed to you an interest in taking up the sport.

- Golf is a great non-contact sport, played outdoors on beautifully landscaped fields.

- Anyone, large or small, old or young, strong or frail, male or female, can play the game.

- Golf teaches some of life's greatest lessons including fair play, etiquette, and discipline.

WHAT AGE SHOULD I GET MY CHILD STARTED IN GOLF?

This is perhaps the most frequently asked question by parents. Stories of Tiger Woods learning the sport from his high chair are popular examples of a very early acquaintance with golf. Tiger's phenomenal golfing prowess, has inspired many parents to introduce their children to this exciting sport at a very young age.

Most young children lack the physical and mental ability to hold or swing a golf club properly until the age of six. The attention span of even a six-year-old is limited. The most effective way of getting children started in golf under the age of six, is to buy inexpensive, plastic golf clubs and balls, and just let them have fun playing with these new tools in your back yard or park. At this stage, it is best not to over coach your child. Children are great at mimicking what you do, so let your child see you hit the plastic ball, and invite them to do the same. Make sure your child is having fun with this new activity. The moment your child loses focus or becomes bored with the sport, it's time to put the clubs away for another day.

ONCE MY CHILD IS READY, THEN WHAT?

The age of six or seven is the time to introduce a metal club to your child. If you have an adult sized putter in the house, you can get that club cut down to your child's size and have the club regripped. Sizing, customizing and regripping clubs can be done at the pro shop of your local golf course. The cost for cutting or sizing a club runs about $10.00 per club, and new grips run anywhere from about $8.00 to $15.00 depending on the quality of grips you choose.

Now is the time to bring your child to the practice green on a golf course to experience the joy of trying to putt the golf ball into the cup. Make up little putting games with them, e.g., the first person to sink 3 putts from a particular distance wins. Take your child to play miniature golf to acquaint them with the game. The key is to create a fun, relaxing atmosphere for your child. Children who are having fun on the golf course and remember it as an enjoyable activity are less likely to abandon the game when its challenges cause frustration.

YOUR CHILD CAN'T PUTT THEIR WAY AROUND THE COURSE – WHAT ELSE DO THEY NEED?

From the age of six upwards, your children are ready to move up to a starter set of golf clubs. The starter set usually consists of a driver, a #3 or #5 fairway wood, a #5, #7 or #9 iron, a pitching and sand wedge, and a putter. Cutting, sizing and regripping old clubs will do in the short run. However, this is not the preferred method once your child is ready for their own set of clubs.

When a club has been shortened, it loses flexibility. Children swing more slowly than adults and a club with a stiff shaft will impair your child's ability to get adequate height on their shots. If your budget precludes purchasing new clubs, check with shops like *Play It Again Sports* or log onto the PGA Foundation Web site "Clubs For Kids" at www.youngamericansgolf.com.

Also check out *kidsklubs*, the ultralight junior golf clubs at www.uskidsgolf.com. You can also search ebay, or your local classified ads for used equipment for your children. A used set of children's clubs from these sources costs around $130.00 and usually contains a driver, #3 wood, two irons, a putter and the golf bag.

If you do decide to buy a new set of clubs for your children, check with the pro at your local golf course to choose the proper clubs for them. The length, shaft flexibility, weight and grip size should all be taken into consideration so that the clubs are designed to match your child's stature and body shape.

THE GOLF CLUBS: The Woods

Here's a look at each of the clubs and what they do:

THE DRIVER, OR #1 WOOD is the largest club in the bag and is used to drive the ball off the tee. It will carry the ball the farthest distance because it has the smallest loft (angle of inclination) and will send the ball on a lower and longer trajectory. It usually has a larger head than the other woods.

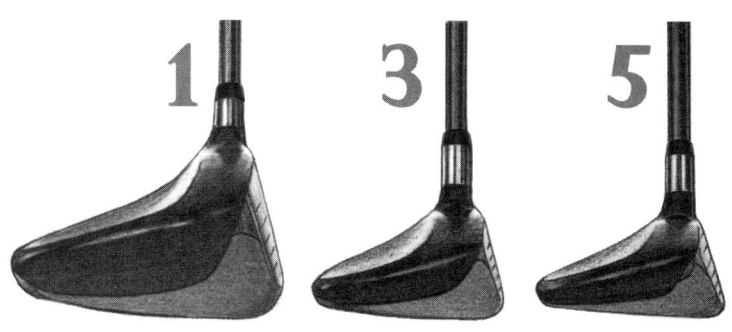

THE FAIRWAY WOODS are so-named because they are designed for use on the fairway, though some golfers use them out of bunkers, heavy grass and even from the fringe on the green. The fairway woods are numbered from 2 through double digits. The higher the number, the greater the loft and usually the less distance the ball will travel.

The #3 wood is usually the second longest club in the bag in terms of the distance it hits the ball and the length of the shaft. The #5 wood is a shorter club and has more loft than the #3 wood, so the ball will go a shorter distance, but will fly higher into the air.

THE GOLF CLUBS: The Long Irons

THE LONG IRONS (#3 and #4) are used to hit the ball long distances because they have a relatively low loft and send the ball in a long low trajectory. Their lower loft makes them more difficult to hit and so they are not usually recommended for young children.

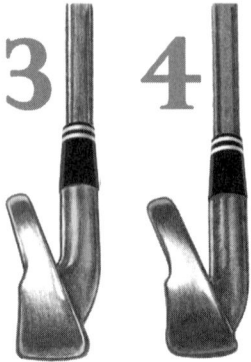

THE MID-IRONS (#5, #6 and #7) are the clubs that your child will use most often to move the ball down the fairway. The lower the number, (like the #5 iron, for instance), the smaller the loft or angle on the clubface, meaning the ball will go low and long. The higher the club (like the #7 iron) the higher the loft/angle, so the ball will go higher into the air, but will travel a shorter distance.

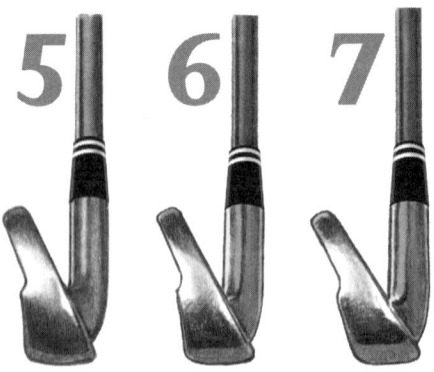

THE GOLF CLUBS: The Short Irons

THE SHORT IRONS (#8, #9 and Wedges) are the clubs that your child will use most often to pitch the ball onto the green. The #8 and #9 irons are used for longer pitches to the greens. The wedges are described below.

THE PITCHING WEDGE is a short club with a large angled loft. It is used to pitch the ball onto the green from about 75 yards. It is also a useful club to pitch your ball high over trees, water or sand. The large loft on a pitching wedge gives the ball a great deal of back-spin so the ball tends to stay on the green once it has landed, without rolling too far away.

THE SAND WEDGE as its name implies, is used to get your ball out of the sand trap. Its bottom flange and its high loft enables it to slide under the ball and lift it out of the bunker. The sand wedge is also used to pitch or chip to the green or hit the ball out of long grass.

THE PUTTER comes in all shapes and sizes and is a personal choice regarding the style and comfort determining your selection. It is a straight faced club designed to roll the ball along the green into the cup. The appropriate length is most important in selecting a putter for your child. The grip end of the putter should come to the top of the trouser inseam.

Every club except the putter, is designed with narrow grooves that run horizontally across the clubface. These grooves allow the ball to spin backwards after you hit it, creating a "backspin" on the ball and causing it to stop where it lands instead of rolling off the green.

19

WHAT OTHER EQUIPMENT DOES MY CHILD NEED?

THE GOLF BAG

A small, sturdy golf bag suitable for your child's age and size will suffice. Some youngsters prefer to carry their clubs rather than use a golf cart, so a light-weight bag that has a shoulder harness is perfect. Some bags also come equipped with metal "legs" to stand the bag upright, making it convenient for the golfer to select their clubs. Make sure the bag contains several zippered compartments to hold all the necessary accessories, and that the zippers are all in working order. The bag should be large enough to adequately hold the size of clubs your child is using. Select an inexpensive bag because children soon outgrow their golf clubs and the bag that houses them. Most sets of children's golf clubs come equipped with their own little golf bag.

GOLF BALLS

Your child will need a dozen or so "experienced" golf balls to carry them through their first round of golf. (Experienced balls are used golf balls that can be purchased at your golf course.) These balls are cheaper than new balls and are ideal for a beginning golfer. Balls are numbered for identification, usually from one to eight, making it easy for your child to recognize their own ball especially when they are playing with several other partners. A small magic-marking pen like the "Sharpie" is a handy tool for your child to use to mark their ball with their initials or any other identifying mark to help recognize their ball.

GOLF TEES

Golf tees appropriate for using a driver as well as an iron or fairway wood off the tee are necessary tools. The less expensive tees are made of wood and break pretty easily, so it's best for your child to carry at least a dozen tees in their golf bag compartment for an 18-hole round of golf. The plastic and brush tees are more expensive, but don't break as often. The larger the club used for driving, the longer the tee. All these tees can be purchased at your golf pro shop or retail golf shops.

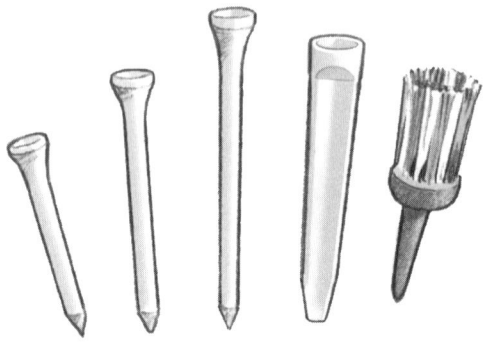

GOLF TOWEL

A small golf towel is very handy to clean any dirt off the ball or golf club. Without access to a towel, your child might use their golf shirt or blouse! The golf towel is equipped with a metal hook, making it convenient to attach the towel onto the golf bag. The ball can only be cleaned before it is set on the tee, and after it has landed on the green and has been marked with a marker.

BALL MARKERS

Once the ball has landed on the green, a marker is placed on the green, identifying the ball's position on the green. Inexpensive, plastic markers can also be purchased at the pro shop.

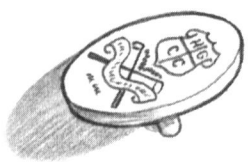

REPAIR TOOL

A repair tool that looks like a
two-pronged fork without the
long handle, is useful for repairing the green after the ball has
landed on it. The repair tool is

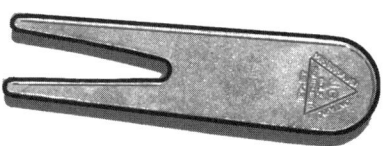

inserted on the side of the decompressed green, while pushing the
grass upward. Patting the green down with the flat end of the putter
helps restore the green to where it was before the ball landed and
punched a hole on the surface.

GOLF UMBRELLA

A golf umbrella is usually larger than a standard umbrella. It helps
keep not only the golfer, but also the golf clubs and bag dry in the
event of a sudden rain shower. An umbrella with a wooden or
graphite shaft is better than one with a metal shaft, as metal conducts
electricity in a lightning storm. More information on lightning storm
awareness is provided in Chapter 5 – Golf Safety.

OTHER NECESSARY ACCESSORIES

Other necessities that can be stored in your child's zippered compartments are water bottles, sun screen, bug spray, a light-weighted jacket
for warmth and protection from the rain, and loose change in case
your child needs something at the half-way house (the little hut located between the 9th and 10th holes) that usually sells beverages
and light snacks.

CLOTHING

Although most youngsters would be more comfortable wearing blue
jeans and a t-shirt to the golf course, this attire is not permitted. Most
courses require that all golfers wear collared golf shirts and shorts no
more than 3 or 4 inches above the knee or cotton pants. Skorts for
girls are also permissible.

GOLF SHOES

Most golf courses require golf shoes equipped with soft spikes, but running shoes are also permissible. Golf shoes can get rather expensive, so if you're on a tight budget, running shoes will do just fine until your children reach an age where their feet have stopped growing, or they can buy the golf shoes themselves.

GOLF SOCKS

Every golf course, it seems, has a sock length regulation, and every ten years or so, this standard seems to change. Some courses prohibit the use of tennis-length or dress socks for men and boys on their courses, and insist on ankle-length socks, or sockettes, whereas other courses have no sock length standards at all. It might be best to check with the pro shop beforehand regarding their sock length policy, and dress accordingly.

GOLF GLOVE

The golf glove helps your child grip the golf club in their hands so that it doesn't slip while they are swinging the club. If your child is right-handed, a left-handed golf glove is needed, and if your child is left-handed, then they will need a right-handed glove. Your pro shop can offer you a range of sizes and prices of gloves for your child, in leather or synthetic.

HAT OR SUN VISOR

A baseball hat or sun visor offers protection from the sun and also blocks out peripheral distractions so your child can better focus their attention on the ball.

Notes

Notes

Chapter 2

Getting Started: Where

NOW THAT WE HAVE ALL THE EQUIPMENT, WHERE DO WE GO FROM HERE?

Head to your neighborhood driving range to let your child hit a bag of balls using their new golf tools. A small bag of balls costs about $4.00; medium bag, $7.00; large bag, $10.00. Some golf courses offer range balls dispensed from a ball machine. Pay for your range balls token at the pro shop. Place the bucket directly under the slot from where the balls are dropped, then drop the token into the machine and wait for the bucket to fill with range balls. On the driving range, safety is probably more important than getting the ball into the air. Make sure your child has lots of space to swing the club. Don't worry about what direction the ball goes. If you're an experienced golfer, you can provide some fundamental golf instruction like grip and stance, but try not to over-direct. Remember that what your child learns in the first few attempts on the driving range can stay with them forever. A small bag of balls is probably a better buy at this stage. It's best to hit just enough balls so that you leave the driving range with a happy, contented child, willing to return another day.

HOW DO I CHOOSE A GOLF COURSE FOR MY CHILD?

This is where careful research can really help your child. If you already belong to a neighborhood golf course, check to see if they have a junior program for your child. Children often feel comfortable knowing their parents are golfing at the same course. If your course does not offer junior programs, visit or go on line to the various golf courses in your community. Investigate and see if they offer instruction and clinics for juniors. Personally meet with the instructors and see if these professionals are suited to your child's personality. Your child needs to relate to the professional in a comfortable way, and if the golf pro does not connect positively with your child, it's time to investigate another golf course. If you or your child feels that things are not progressing well, ask other parents or junior golfers for referrals in order to find the right golf pro for your child.

WHAT SHOULD I LOOK FOR WHEN CHOOSING A GOLF PRO FOR MY CHILD?

Look for a pro's accreditation. Lessons should be performed by pros with PGA, (Professional Golf Association), LPGA (Ladies Professional Golf Association), GTF (Golf Teachers Federation) and for Canadians, CPGA (Canadian Professional Golf Association) accreditation. Find out if the golf pro is involved in any junior programs. Apart from formal teaching requirements, you should look for a golf pro who is enthusiastic about working with children. Children learn better when the instructor keeps the golf lessons fun, exciting and upbeat.

WHAT LESSONS SHOULD I ENROLL MY CHILD IN?

This is probably one of the most important sections in this book. Choosing golf lessons for your children can be very confusing. There are golf clinics, golf academies, golf camps, private lessons, semi-private lessons, short-term programs, long-term programs, competitions, and about a million Internet sites for "junior golf" that can leave a parent feeling completely baffled. The moment you open one golf Internet site, a dozen more links are offered for you to open in order to get the information you're looking for. As a parent, I went through the very same confusing, time-consuming path trying to find the correct route to get my own kids involved in golf.

In researching information for this book, we visited hundreds of Internet sites and links, and thoroughly investigated golf courses and schools. Lessons, duration of programs, targeted age groups, and costs vary depending on the individual school and program. What follows is a one-stop-shopping summary of the many golf lessons, programs and schools that are offered, as well as the costs, from the fundamental beginning golf program to a golf professional readiness program (if that's the route you and your child wish to take) and everything else in between. A section listing many of the golf schools, with their Web site addresses and phone numbers, is included in Chapter 12.

INTRODUCTION TO GOLF PROGRAM

There are many great beginner golf programs available to junior golfers. From ages six and up, where children have little or no experience, enroll your child in an "Introduction to Golf" junior program at a course both you and your child have chosen. Many golf courses provide free golf clubs to children who do not own a set of clubs. Most junior programs are offered in groups from about 8 to 12 children, both boys and girls, with 2 professional golf instructors per group. The group program is a great way to start for a beginner golfer. The lessons are fun and learning in a group setting eliminates the fear of being singled out on a one-on-one basis. The fundamental golf skills are taught at this level: stance, posture, grip, objective, putting, chipping and the full swing. Each lesson is about an hour in length, and the program runs for 4 weeks. The cost is around $100 per child.

PRIVATE/SEMI-PRIVATE GOLF LESSONS

If your child prefers a more personalized approach to instruction, most golf courses offer private and semi-private lessons. Meet with the pro beforehand to ensure that your child responds positively to the pro's personality. Make sure the pro is enthusiastic about the sport and has experience in teaching golf to juniors. Lessons can run anywhere from 30 minutes to an hour in length, and can be offered either in individual sessions, or packages of three to five sessions. Lessons can cost anywhere from $40.00 for a 30 minute lesson, $100 for three 45 minute sessions, $150 for five 30 minute sessions or $250 for five 60 minute sessions, depending on the golf course. If your child has a buddy who is also interested in learning to golf, semi-private lessons are also available. Some golf courses offer one hour semi-private lessons to juniors for about $40 per student.

INTERMEDIATE GOLF PROGRAM

This program is for the intermediate golfer with some golf experience, all ages, both boys and girls. This program involves a more in-depth and personalized form of instruction. Additional skills beyond the fundamental ones taught in the beginner's program are alignment, pitching, sand play and course management. These are also offered in groups of 12 or more children, with 2 instructors, one hour in duration for 4 weeks at approximately $100 per child.

JUNIOR ELITE PROGRAM

Junior elite programs are offered to children 13 to 16 years of age who have progressed through elementary golf lessons. These programs prepare the junior golfers for tournaments. Advanced techniques with video analysis, swing related drills and physical exercises are included. The elite programs are usually one-and-a-half-hour sessions, one day a week for 4 weeks. The cost is around $150 per student.

JUNIOR GOLF CAMPS-BEGINNER AND INTERMEDIATE

Golf camps for juniors are offered for golfers aged 6 to 14. The children are grouped according to age and skill level. The difference between a golf program and a golf camp is the duration and intensity of the program. Golf camps usually consist of 5 consecutive days of intensive instruction including putting, chipping, irons, woods, rules and etiquette. They usually run from Monday to Friday, 8:00 a.m. to 3:00 p.m., lunch included. The cost of junior golf camps runs anywhere from $120 to $400.00 per student depending on the school and their program.

JUNIOR ELITE GOLF CAMP

This week long camp runs from Monday to Friday for junior golfers aged 13 to 16. The elite camp usually consists of no more than 6 students per camp. The students are given 20 hours of golf instruction including lessons on the short game, the mental game, and tournament preparation. Students play 18 holes of golf each day with competitions, video lessons, and unlimited practice balls. Lunch and snacks are included. The cost for the week-long junior elite golf camp is around $900 per student.

GOLF SUMMER CAMPS-JUNIOR SHORT TIME WEEKLY BOARDING/NON-BOARDING

These summer camps are offered on a weekly or multi-weekly, boarding-in or commuting basis, for children aged 8 to 18. Golf instruction includes the short game, full swing, computer-video analysis, fitness instruction and sport psychology, as well as on-course instruction, unlimited range balls and daily rounds of golf. Students participate in a co-educational instructional golf program and are grouped by age and ability. The five day/six night golf program includes daily instruction Monday through Friday, meals and accommodation from approximately $1200 to $1500 per week, depending on the school. Subtract about $300 per week for non-boarding, commuting students. You can enroll your child from one to four weeks in the summer.

JUNIOR FULL-TIME BOARDING/NON-BOARDING-ONE YEAR GOLF PROGRAM

Full time semester programs run from September to May for children aged 12 to 18, grades 6 to 12. Students attend school in the morning (either a school that is part of the golf academy, or a private school affiliated with the golf academy). The afternoon is dedicated to perfecting the golf swing, as well as mental and physical conditioning. On weekends, the students test their skills in tournaments geared to the individual's level. This program provides serious juniors the chance to take their games to the highest possible level. The cost for this one-year golf program varies from school to school, but expect to pay anywhere from $30,000 to $46,000 per student per year, which includes academic schooling, accommodation, meals, and golf instruction.

POST-SECONDARY GOLF PROGRAM

If your child has attended a junior full-time golf academy, and is interested in attending a college geared to their golf training, a golf academy professional will assist the student in selecting an appropriate college. They will work with your student's golf coach to create a recruitment video, as well as liaison with your student's academic teachers to ensure that they meet the academic requirements (SAT's, GPA's, etc.) for college placement. It is helpful too to check with your child's chosen college, to determine if your child is eligible for an athletic scholarship.

There are other institutions that also cater to post-secondary golf students designed for aspiring professional golfers who have completed their high school education and are looking for an intensive golf training program for the purpose of preparing for professional tournament play. These post secondary golf programs run anywhere from one week to six months of instruction and cost from $175 for one week to $1500 for the six months.

POST GRADUATE GOLF PROGRAMS

The goal of the post grad program is to prepare the amateur, professional and college golfers for the rigors of professional competition. Technique, pre-competition readiness, competitive golf tournaments, mental and physical training are offered in this program. The Junior Tour Prep Program, including boarding, costs approximately $7500 per month. This package includes golf instruction, meals and accommodations. Non-boarding students pay approximately $6500 per month.

DOES MY CHILD NEED TO ATTEND GOLF SCHOOL IN ORDER TO BECOME A GOLF PRO?

Not every family has the means to send their children to golf academies. If your child has been golfing as a junior and is interested in a career as a golf pro by the time they reach high school, have them enroll in their high school golf team. If your child's high school tournament scoring average is in the low 70s, colleges will find them. If your child has a high school tournament scoring average in the low 80s, they will have to locate the colleges themselves, but there is still a place for play. For golfers in high school who shoot in the 70s, there are many national junior golf tournament associations. This is where they should be playing in order to reach their true potential. (See Chapter 11 on Associations and Chapter 12 on Schools for Web site addresses.)

Notes

Chapter 3

Getting into the Swing

THE FUNDAMENTAL GOLF SWING

Although this book is not intended to offer instruction, as that is best offered by the golf professional, there are a few fundamental guidelines that every golfer follows in order to produce a half-decent golf shot. In fact, there are three fundamental tips to consider in order to execute a good golf swing:

- the grip
- the stance
- the alignment or posture

The *grip* refers to the placement of your hands on the club, and will determine the direction of the club at impact with the ball. There are three types of grips – the baseball or 10 finger grip (which is best for very young children until they are stronger), the interlocking grip, and the overlapping grip. Your golf pro will advise your child which grip is best for them.

Baseball Grip	**Interlocking Grip**	**Overlapping Grip**

In the baseball grip, one hand is placed above the other. This grip is common with beginners but less popular with low handicappers.	In the interlocking grip, the baby finger of the top hand fits between the index finger and the middle finger of the bottom hand. This helps the hands swing as a unit.	In the overlapping grip, the baby finger of the top hand rests in the slot between the index and middle finger of the bottom hand, enabling the hands to swing more fluidly as a unit.

The *stance* is the posture or positioning of the body as you address the ball. Your golf pro will teach your child to bend at the waist, feet shoulder-width apart, with the front foot pointing a little towards the target, a slight bend at the knees and arms hanging straight down.

The *alignment* is simply how you aim the club and body to the target. Your child's feet should be lined up parallel to the direction they wish to hit the ball.

Stance   Alignment

PRACTICE, PRACTICE AND MORE PRACTICE

Now that you have chosen the appropriate golf lessons for your child, it is very important to practice all the techniques they learned in their programs on the driving range. This is also a great time for parent and child to bond together while hitting a bucket of balls at the practice range. Remember to do some warm-up exercises with your child prior to hitting range balls. Take a club in your hands and reach up to the sky with outstretched arms. Stretch gently from side to side with your club, then gently bend downward to get your lower body ready for golf.

Warm-up Exercises

Remember to keep the practice round just long enough for your child to hone the fundamentals they've learned in their golf programs, but short enough that they leave the range happy and willing to return another day. Be positive, encourage your child and let them grow with confidence in what they learned in their golf lessons with the pro. Your child will leave the range feeling good, and that is important. If the experience is fun and positive, they will want to come back.

Practicing at the Driving Range

Practicing on the driving range helps the child improve their swing technique while discovering the distance each club can hit the ball. The practice range is equipped with colored flags placed at various distances on the range. A pole or marker, placed at the area from where your child will be hitting the balls, indicates how far away each flag is positioned. When your child finally tries out their game on the course, they will know exactly what club to choose for each distance needed to get their ball to the green.

TAKING YOUR GAME TO THE COURSE

Once your child feels comfortable with lessons from the golf pro, has warmed up and practiced on the driving range and is eager to try their skill on the golf course, a nine-hole executive course is an ideal starting point. A par three course where all holes are less than 200 yards is a much more relaxed, non-threatening and easier course for beginning junior golfers. Nine holes of golf on a short or executive course usually takes less than two hours to play. An 18-hole regulation size golf course takes at least four hours to play and a beginning junior golfer may get discouraged playing a long, time-consuming game of golf. If you can't find a short course in your neighborhood, modify the regular golf course near you. Your child can tee up the ball down the fairway, anywhere from 200 to 100 yards out from the green and start from there.

Although greens fees vary from course to course, the average cost of greens fees for nine holes of golf on an executive course is approximately $16.00 Monday to Friday; $18.00 Saturday, Sunday and holidays. Power carts usually cost $15.00 and $3.00 for a pull cart.

Greens fees for 18 holes of regulation golf for juniors cost about $40.00 Monday to Thursday; $50.00 on weekends and holidays. The cost usually drops if you choose to play golf after 3:00 p.m. Some golf courses offer family night golfing – about 2 and a half hours before dark – and costs about $17.00 per member. Check with your local golf course for rates and times.

ANATOMY OF THE GOLF COURSE:

A regulation size golf course consists of 18 holes, and of these holes, some of them will be par 3's, par 4's and par 5's. This means that it should take you one drive to reach the green and two putts to get the ball into the cup for a par 3; one drive, one fairway shot to reach the green, and two putts for a par 4 hole, and one drive, two fairway shots to the green and two putts to get the ball into the cup for a par 5. In order to score par golf, it would take exactly 72 strokes for the entire round of 18 holes.

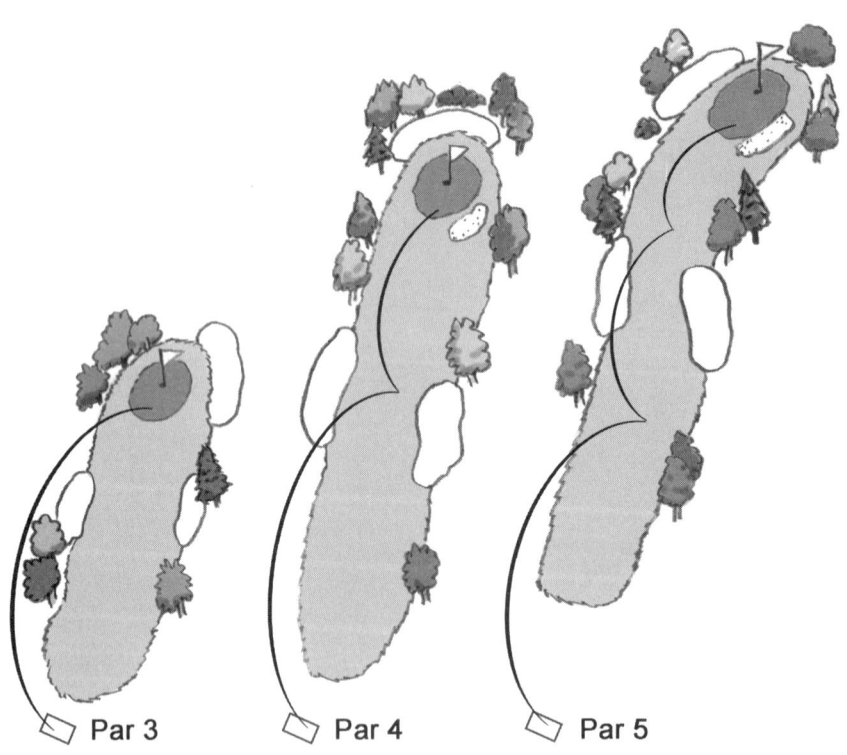

Par 3   Par 4   Par 5

FROM TEE TO GREEN

Here's what a typical golf hole looks like.

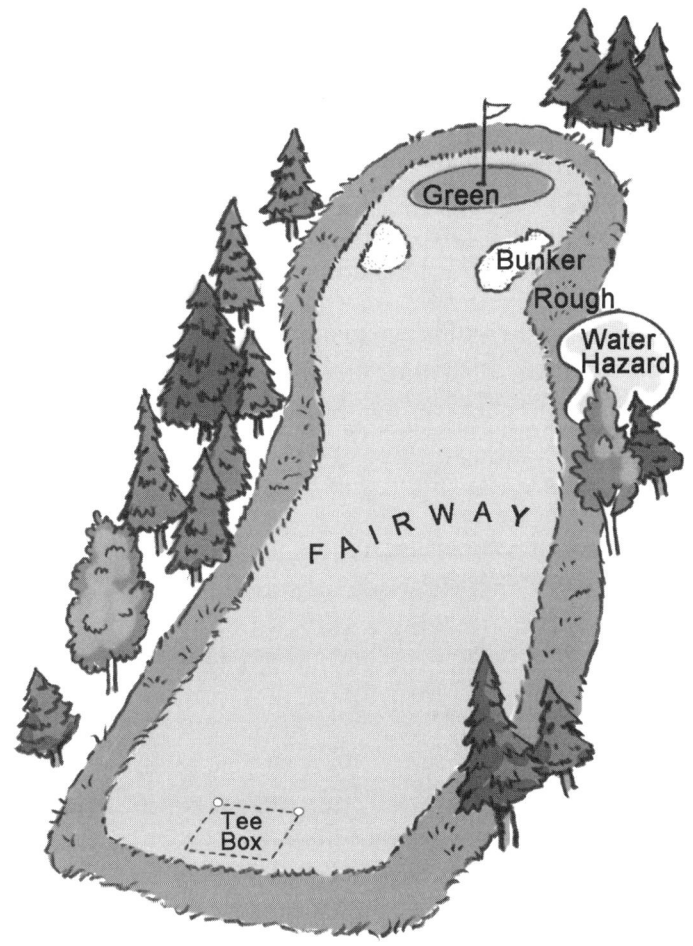

Obviously, the object of the game of golf is to get the ball from the tee into the hole on the green in as few strokes as possible. In regulation golf, the course consists of 18 holes, and the executive or short course consists of 9 holes.

Each hole consists of: The Tee Box   The Fairway   The Rough
                        The Hazards   The Bunkers   The Green

Each of these is described in the pages that follow.

The *tee box* is a rectangular area of grass with one or more pairs of color-coded markers positioned a few yards apart. A golfer must drive the ball from between the colored markers that correspond to his or her level of play. For example, an adult male who strikes the ball a long distance, might choose to play from the blue-colored markers, while an average male golfer, will usually choose to play from the white markers. Females, unless they are professional caliber, usually tee off from the red markers (also called "forward tees"). Junior golfers also hit their tee shots from the red tees, but as young males age and progress in their golf game, they typically move back and tee off from the white or blue colored tee boxes.

The *fairway* is the stretch of grass that leads to the green. It is sometimes framed by a row of mature trees on either side. The fairway consists of grass that is cut to a height of one to two inches. It is advantageous to drive the ball onto the fairway in order to ensure a clear, easy passage for the ball to approach the green.

The *rough* is the area of grass on either side of the fairway. There is little wonder why this area is called "the rough". The grass is usually three to six inches high, making it difficult to hit a good shot. The trees lining the fairway offer an additional challenge for the golfer trying to approach the green from a position off the fairway.

The *hazards* are sometimes a small body of water like a pond, stream or lake, although not all golf holes have these kinds of hazards. A ball that lands in a water hazard will likely be lost and the golfer will be penalized a stroke for their unfortunate shot, so it is wise to avoid the hazard as much as you can.

The *bunkers* or *sand traps* that are situated on the fairway are designed to prevent the golfer from reaching the green on the approach shot. These types of bunkers are usually large but not deep. The sand is usually granular in texture, and it is reasonably easy to hit the ball from this area. The bunkers surrounding or protecting the green, however, are quite different. They can be deep and very challenging. The sand is usually very soft – almost a cake-mix consistency, which makes it difficult to explode a ball and control its flight.

The *green* is the final destination of the ball on each hole. It consists of a patch of closely cut grass, with a six foot flagstick or "pin" in the cup or hole.

KEEPING SCORE

It is important that you not keep score while your child is just learning the game of golf. Score-keeping often undermines the fun of shot making and experimentation.

The scorecard is equipped with lots of useful information, like the length of each hole and the distance from various points on the fairway. This helps a golfer determine what club to select to reach the green and the scorecard can be used for this purpose. Children tend to be competitive and are often intimidated if their scores don't measure up to their partners' scores. In the early stages, maintain the game as a recreational sport rather than a competitive event. Once your child has grown and matured to a point where they are confident about keeping score, then the scorecard can be introduced into their game. You can also be creative in score-keeping with a young golfer. Increase the par for your child by 2 strokes. As the child grows and their game improves, the par can be set lower. When scoring has become part of your child's game, honest score-keeping is imperative, but we will revisit this topic in Chapter 6, *Etiquette* and Chapter 7, *Values*.

ANATOMY OF A SCORECARD

Deciphering a scorecard can be a little difficult. Below, we see a sample scorecard with some notes that may help you record your child's scores when they are ready to set personal targets.

Front Nine Holes

	Slope/Rating	Hole	1	2	3	4	5	6	7	8	9	OUT
Hole number →												
	124/71.4 → BLACK	397	135	425	195	552	541	420	214	390	3269
	122/70.5 GOLD	363	135	390	185	519	541	410	199	390	3132
	119/69.1 BLUE	354	129	369	173	498	499	400	188	371	2981
	112/67.4 → WHITE	323	119	363	164	446	456	354	175	362	2752
	HDCP MEN	9	17	3	15	7	1	5	13	11	
	SEAN										
	AARON										
	+/−										
	PAR MEN/LADIES	4	3	4	3	5	5	4	3	4	35
	+/−										
	SHANNON										
	MELANIE										
	109/66.6 RED	294	109	289	139	440	450	298	88	345	2443
	HDCP LADIES	7	15	11	13	3	1	9	17	5	

Hole number →

Tees you can play from to match your skill level – black tees are the longest and red tees the shortest.

Men's Handicap Holes are rated by difficulty from the most difficult, #1, to the easiest, #18.

Area where the score on each hole is entered

names of golfers

Par = expected number of strokes for a very competent golfer.

Women's Handicap Holes are rated by difficulty from the most difficult, #1, to the easiest, #18.

The first column in the scorecard gives the course slope/rating which indicates its level of difficulty relative to other courses. A rating of 71.4 for the gold tees indicates that from those tees, the course plays slightly easier than a course with a standard rating of 72.

Back Nine Holes

10	11	12	13	14	15	16	17	18	IN	TOT.	Ladies		
548	434	380	393	185	500	395	419	189	3443	6712	Slope/Rating		
535	406	380	393	158	500	369	404	180	3325	6457	136/76.4		
522	379	356	352	145	490	359	392	170	3165	6146	129/74.5		
473	313	345	306	129	478	326	355	162	2887	5639	122/72.2		
2	6	14	10	16	4	12	8	18			HDCP	NET	NAME
5	4	4	4	3	5/4	4	4	3	36/35	71/70			
468	308	293	295	103	351	320	345	147	2626	5069	114/69.1		
2	8	14	12	18	4	10	6	16					

← Total score for 18 holes

Your personal handicap is the number of strokes you receive from a 0-handicap golfer. To obtain your net score subtract your handicap from your total score.

49

USING THE SCORECARD FOR COURSE MANAGEMENT

The scorecard has lots of information that can help you decide where to aim your tee shot or what club to select. Often small illustrations on the card show the shape of the fairway and the green of each hole, revealing the hazards and the distances to them. The scorecard may show that a particular hole is designed as a "dog-leg left," meaning that it is shaped like the numeral 7. This might prompt you to hit your tee shot with a fairway wood to reach the corner of the fairway without rolling into the rough beyond the fairway, then continue left on the fairway until you reach the green.

The locations of the hazards and the distances shown on the scorecard help the golfer select the appropriate club for a particular shot. Careful consideration of this useful information to plan shots is an important part of managing your golf game.

HANDICAPS

As a novice golfer, your child will not have a handicap number. The handicap is a measure of a golfer's average score above par. On a golf course with a par of 72, a golfer who regularly shoots around 72, is said to be "playing par (or scratch) golf" – something most golfers are itching to achieve.

A golfer who scores 92 on average is playing 20 strokes over par on a course with an 18-hole rating of 72 and is assigned a handicap of 20. This is the number that the golfer enters on the space on the scorecard called "handicap". When two golfers of different levels of skill play competitively, the less skilled player is able to deduct the difference in their handicaps from his or her score. The handicap is golf's way of "leveling the links."

As a golfer's game improves, their handicap number comes down. Most golf courses have computers available for their golf members to enter their scores. The computer records and automatically updates the handicap each time a score is entered into the computer. Golfers are expected to enter all accurate scores for all games to ensure fairness, particularly when competing in tournaments.

Notes

Notes

Chapter 4

Playing by the Rules

RULES, RULES AND MORE RULES:

Golf, like all sports, comes equipped with its own set of rules. In fact, golf clearly has more than its share of rules. There are lots of books out there on the rules of golf, and it might be worth your while to invest in a book of rules for junior golfers. There are no umpires or referees in the game of golf, and it is up to the individual golfer to keep an honest score and know some of the fundamental rules of golf. It is wise to acquaint your child with accurate score-keeping and the rules of golf as early as possible. Developing the habit of reporting an honest score in golf is an important step toward building integrity. Here are just a few of the more significant rules that your child should know.

1. A golfer can have up to, but no more than, 14 clubs in their bag. There is a two-stroke penalty for breaking this rule which is strictly enforced if your child is involved in a tournament.

2. The ball must be teed up within or behind the two colored markers on the teeing surface. A two-stroke penalty is assessed a golfer who tees the ball forward of the tee blocks or anywhere outside of the tee blocks.

3. The ball must be played where it lies. If the ball rests in the rough, beside a tree, or even in a divot on the fairway, the golfer cannot move the ball in order to get a better (preferred) lie. Strict observance of this rule is the ultimate test of honesty. (This is where real character-building comes in – more about values and character-building in the upcoming chapters.)

4. When a ball enters a hazard (water or sand bunker) the golfer is prohibited from "grounding" the club, i.e., touching the ground or grass surface in a practice swing. The practice swing must be executed without touching the ground. A one stroke penalty is assessed if the golfer grounds a club in the hazard area.

5. A golfer who hits a tee shot into the rough, or any other area where the ball is not immediately visible, has 5 minutes to hunt for it. If the ball is not found within that time, the golfer must play a provisional ball (a second ball struck from the tee) and add an extra stroke to the score. If the ball is lost after a fairway shot, the golfer must return to where the ball was before it was lost and hit the ball again. A stroke for the lost ball is added to the golfer's score – a cruel penalty considering the cost of the ball!

6. If a tee shot enters a water hazard (marked by yellow stakes) the next shot must be played from the "drop zone" – a specially designated "tee box" usually situated a little closer to the green. If the ball is retrieved from a water hazard, it may be dropped two club lengths from where it entered the water, but no closer to the hole. If it is lost in the water, the same option applies. Both conditions incur a one-stroke penalty.

7. If a ball comes to rest in a lateral hazard (marked by red stakes) it may be dropped two club lengths from the point of entry, but no closer to the hole. A one-stroke penalty is added to the score.

8. A ball can be considered unplayable anywhere on the golf course, except when it goes into the water and a one-stroke penalty is assessed. An unplayable lie occurs when the ball rests in an area that is determined to be an impossible position from which to strike the ball, c.g., stuck in the fork of a tree. In such a case, the ball may be dropped two club lengths from where it landed, but no closer to the hole. A one-stroke penalty is assessed.

There are dozens of other rules of golf, and as your child gains more experience with the game, the fundamental rules outlined above will become second nature. Many golf courses offer clinics specifically designed for teaching these rules, and if your child is ready to learn, these clinics can be a good investment. To enhance your child's enjoyment of the game, use discretion on enforcing rules. The key is to achieve a balance between applying the fundamental rules of golf and having fun on the golf course.

Notes

Chapter 5

Golf Safety

GOLF SAFETY

This is a very important chapter in the book, and one you should review with your children to ensure their safety and the safety of others on the golf course. Though golf is considered a relatively safe sport (especially compared to sports like football or hockey) there are some hazards, other than those designed to raise your score, that your child should be aware of.

Only one person should be on the tee at a time. All other golfers should stand away from the tee and behind the golfer. Standing near a golfer executing practice swings or an actual shot is a recipe for disaster. Also the golfer addressing a ball on the tee should routinely check to ensure that there are no other golf partners in their way before swinging the club. On the course, a good rule of thumb to remember is to keep at least three club lengths' distance from your playing partners, and never aim at anyone. A ball traveling at a fast speed can kill!

One of the most important precautions to stress is to make sure the golfers in the group ahead are out of range before attempting a shot. Every year, people are injured by an impatient golfer who laments, "I didn't think I could hit it that far!" If there is a chance of reaching the golfers playing ahead, it's vitally important to wait until they are out of range – even when encouraged by fellow golfers to go for it. Waiting before hitting a shot also means never hitting a shot to the green until the group ahead has replaced the flag into the hole and has safely left the green.

All golfers know that errant shots are part of the game. As soon as a golfer realizes that he has launched a missile in someone else's direction it is important for the golfer (and/or the fellow golfers) to shout "fore" as loud as possible to attract the attention of those in the target zone. This gives them a "heads up" so they can protect themselves. The word "fore" is the golfer's version of the combat cry, "grenade!"

Practicing these rules will enable your child to have a pleasant and safe round of golf.

Review these important instructions with your child to ensure their safety and the safety of others if they find themselves in a lightning storm.

1. Immediately seek shelter away from water;
2. If your shoes have metal spikes, remove the shoes immediately;
3. If the course's warning system sounds, take cover;
4. If possible, get off the course and find a designated lightning shelter;
5. Stay away from your golf cart, clubs, and surrounding water;
6. Do not stand under a tree, especially a solitary tree in the open;
7. Avoid close contact with others. Spread out 15-20 feet apart;
8. Avoid open spaces;
9. Seek ditches, trenches or low ground if shelter is not available;
10. If you can hear thunder, you are within striking distance of a lightning storm. Seek safe shelter immediately.

Notes

Chapter 6

Etiquette

Golf has always been considered a "genteel" sport, characterized by good will, fellowship and mutual respect. Listed below are some general guidelines of golf etiquette with which your children should be acquainted.

1. Always try to arrive at the golf course at least a half hour prior to your tee time. This will allow your children plenty of time to check in with the pro shop to announce their arrival, change from their street shoes to golf shoes, and maybe even hit a small bucket of balls for practice before heading off to the first tee. Often, the pro shop will tell you if there's been a cancelation, so your tee time might be moved ahead a few minutes.

2. "Ready golf" is a term that your children will encounter as they continue to play golf. This phrase means that the first person who is ready with their ball, tee and driver, should stand up at the tee, and proceed to tee off. Ready golf helps to speed up the pace of the game – an increasingly important issue on most public golf courses as the game grows in popularity. Four hours is generally accepted as a reasonable time to play 18 holes. As the time increases beyond four hours, patience begins to wear thin and frustration sets in.

   Each golfer is responsible for being ready on the tee, hitting their tee shot, and walking promptly to where their ball has landed. Golfers are expected to keep up with the golfers ahead. If there is a full one or two-hole gap between you and the golfers ahead, then it's time to pick up the pace. No one expects your children to run through their golf game, but rather to strive for a good steady pace. If some golfers behind are playing at a faster speed, it is an expected courtesy to let those players "play through".

3. When another golfer is preparing to hit a shot, it is polite to stay quiet. Observing this rule is relatively easy for most golfers, but children and chatterboxes often find the temptation to speak, laugh or break the silence, unbearably irresistible.

4. Perhaps the most difficult rule of etiquette for most golfers to observe is restraint when a shot goes awry. Shouting expletives, complaining and throwing clubs are unacceptable behaviors.

5. When a golfer's ball lands on another fairway, the golfers on that hole have precedence and the right to play first. Once they have hit their ball down their own fairway, the trespassing golfer may then proceed to execute a shot.

6. Shots from the fairway, especially those hit with the high irons, often create a minor crater (called a "divot") in the fairway. Taking divots is natural and often desirable, but replacing the divot is a necessary part of golf course maintenance. To replace a divot the golfer retrieves the grass, roots and all, and places it in the bare spot left behind. Stomping gently on it with the shoe, helps the grass replant itself. On many golf courses where the ground is very sandy, replacing the divot is not recommended. Instead, the golfer is given a small container containing sand and seed that is poured into the hole left by the divot. This enables the grass to regenerate.

7. Golfers are expected to watch where their partners have hit their shots so they can help them locate their ball. This will also help to pick up the speed of play. If a ball is lost, take no more than 5 minutes to look for it.

8. When a ball leaves a mark on the delicate putting green, it is expected that the golfer will repair the green, preferably using the little fork-like repair tool. By gently digging with the tool on the side of the indented area, pushing the grass back upwards, and tapping it down with the putter or shoe, the golfer maintains the integrity of the putting surface.

9. After hitting a ball out of a sand bunker, a golfer is expected to rake all footprints leaving the area ready for the next golfer.

10. Golfers, when on the green, try to avoid walking or standing on a partner's putting line (the line between a partner's ball and the hole). It is good etiquette to walk around a partner's line to ensure a clean, flat surface for putting the ball into the cup.

11. To maintain a "ready-golf" pace, golfers usually place their golf bag or cart alongside the green, heading towards the next hole. Placing a bag on the green (or driving a cart close to the green) is to be avoided because it damages the fragile grass.

12. Golfers mark their scores after moving to the next tee – not while still on the green. This allows the following players to hit their ball to the green, thereby speeding up the pace of play.

13. Recognizing the importance of maintaining a well-manicured course, most golfers try to leave the course in good shape. That means not only repairing greens and replacing divots, but also putting trash into the trash bins located on every tee. Keeping the course neat, tidy and repaired ensures that the course will always be in great shape for every golfer.

The final message in this chapter on etiquette is to treat all players the same way you yourself would like to be treated.

Notes

Chapter 7

Values

GREAT VALUES DERIVED FROM THE GAME OF GOLF

Parents whose children have taken up the game of golf can feel a sense of pride in their sons' and daughters' choice because these youngsters have already demonstrated outstanding character traits. Golf, for the longest time, has been known as the "old man's sport". Thankfully, newer members on the golf scene like Tiger Woods and Paula Creamer are helping to change this outlook by giving the sport a much more exciting reputation. Here is a list of great values your children will obtain simply by taking up the game of golf:

Friendship – Golf is not a sport that every child gravitates to. Life-long friendships will be derived through golf because of this common interest.

Honesty – There are no referees or umpires determining the fairness of the sport. In golf, you are your only scorekeeper. If you cheat on your score, you only cheat yourself.

Sportsmanship – Respect for the game and the rules, and winning and losing gracefully shows great maturity and good sportsman-like behavior.

Respect – In golf, a show of respect for the game, yourself, your partners and the traditions of the game are enforced.

Confidence – Golf is not an easy sport to learn, but as your child becomes more experienced, confidence will grow. With confidence your child's ability will also improve. This confidence in the sport will also spill over to their confidence in life.

Responsibility – Each player must be accountable for their own behavior and actions on the course, from keeping an honest scorecard, to personal conduct, and etiquette.

Perseverance – As noted earlier, golf is not an easy sport. In order to succeed, perseverance is paramount. In fact, perseverance is even more important than innate talent. When asked how he developed his game to become the greatest golfer of his era, Ben Hogan replied, "I dug it out of the ground." It was in reference to his legendary dedication to constant practice. Acquiring such unrelenting perseverance, especially in the face of adversity, is a value that will serve your child well, both on and off the golf course.

Courtesy – Golf has always been known as the "gentleman's" or "gentlewoman's" sport. Courteous behavior towards your partners is encouraged in golf. In life, as in golf, such courtesy is perceived as self respect and a respect for others.

Judgment – The practice of good judgment plays a dominant role in the game of golf. Deciding which club to use, determining the type of shot to hit and what part of the green to aim for, are all part of what golfers refer to as *course management.* Making these decisions, based on wind direction, turf conditions and hazard locations, and living with the results of these decisions, are powerful preparations for decision-making in life.

One of golf's most treasured contributions to its players is the character development and life-enhancing values it imparts. Parents who involve their children in this game at an early age and impart these values not only serve the personal interests of their children, but they also contribute to the moral fabric of our future society.

Notes

Notes

Chapter 8

Frequently Asked Questions (That we haven't addressed)

Although we attempted to address in this book, most of the topics parents would like to know in order to get their children successfully started in golf, this "frequently asked questions" section is included to ensure that the most popular golfing concerns are considered.

Q. Should my children be involved in an exercise program to improve their muscles used in golf?

A. Most golf instructors agree that the most significant limitations they see with golf students are stability, strength and flexibility. Although each child is built differently, and because young bodies are still growing, it is advised that if you do enroll your child in a golf fitness program, that it be properly geared to their specific needs. Juniors should not be using old or outdated body building routines for golf fitness. Focus on the larger trunk muscles as a priority for postural development. A strong base of support will offer great results for a lifetime. Always make time for proper rest and recovery in order for your child to grow and develop properly. Alternate exercises for different parts of the body and change exercises frequently to avoid accumulated fatigue on any specific area.

Q. Are there any statistical data available that compare the percentage of active adult golfers who attended structured golf programs as junior golfers versus those who golfed as juniors, but didn't take professional lessons?

A. According to the National Golf Foundation, adults 19–34 who were exposed to golf through a structured junior program are playing 50% more rounds of golf compared to adults in the same age group who were exposed to the game as a child but not through a structured program. Of every 10 children exposed to the game through a structured program, 6 will be active adult golfers. Of every 10 children exposed to the game as a child but not through a structured program, 3 will be active adult golfers.

Q. Both my husband and I play golf and would like our two-year-old to start golfing too. Can my husband and I teach him a few lessons or is he too young?

A. At this young age, try not to over teach your child. Instead, concentrate on safety with a plastic club and ball. Set up some simple guidelines concerning the direction to hit the ball and when and where to swing safely. Teach your child to keep both hands together and to always have their dominant hand as the bottom hand on the grip. A simple ten finger (baseball) grip will do at this stage. Some young children may not have established right or left hand dominance yet. If your child continually switches the grip and attempts to swing left handed, then get a left handed club. Children this age can also be taught about feet positioning. Have your child try to keep their feet about shoulder width apart to keep them from moving when they swing. Allow them always to have fun with the sport.

Q. How can I tell if my child has potential as a golfer?

A. When looking for potential in junior golfers, remember that each junior is going to grow and learn at different rates. Some junior golfers don't score as well simply because they can't hit the ball as far as other kids their age and size. Don't just look at their scores. Watch how they play the game, see how they chip and putt and look at their shot selection. Many juniors understand the game instantly, while most kids are just trying to hit the ball as far as they can. That is a sign of real potential. Another clue to look for is poise. How do they handle themselves under pressure? Are they mature and restrained or easily angered and frustrated?

As a junior golfer gets older, tournaments become more important. If your child is interested in competing in tournaments, potential to be a good golfer begins to show at these small events. If the junior does well and likes it, the potential is there. The stress of competitions is not for everyone.

Q. My child has a physical disability. Do you think golf is an ideal sport for my child?

A. Golf is a sport that can be adapted to those with disabilities very easily, for two reasons: first, it is a game that pits the golfer against the course with a handicapping system that enables golfers to compete equally; second, the game is played at a pace that does not place undue physical stress on most disabled persons. The golf swing is executed from a standing position, thereby eliminating the running, jumping and other motor skills that severely prohibit most people with disabilities from participating in the sport. In golf, a disabled person can hit a satisfying shot, experiencing the thrill and sense of accomplishment that any other person without disabilities experiences.

Q. My daughter is interested in taking golf lessons but is not comfortable in a co-education program. Are there any golf programs available for girls only?

A. Clearly, there are not as many girls-only golf programs as there are co-educational or boys' programs. The reason is simply that there have not been as many young girls interested in the sport till recently. The tide is changing as more and more young girls are watching golfers like Paula Creamer, Lorena Ochoa and Annika Sorenstam on the LPGA tour. Check with your community golf course to see if they offer girls-only golf instruction. If they do not, then make a wider search by investigating golf camps in your state or province. Organizations like the *LPGA-USGA Girls Golf* provide opportunities for young girls to play golf in a girls-only environment, and they offer programs and camps throughout the United States. In Canada, the RCGA Girls Club offers opportunities exclusively for girls.

Notes

Chapter 9

Golf Terminology

Here is a list of some of the more common terms used in golf. As your children continue to play, these terms will become quite familiar to them.

ACE – A hole in one.

ADDRESS – The positioning of the body in relation to the ball prior to the swing. A player is said to have "addressed" the ball when they have taken their stance and grounded their club.

ALIGNMENT – When the body is in a position to swing the club, in relation to the target.

APPROACH – A shot to the green from anywhere except the teeing area.

APRON – An area of closely mown grass that surrounds the green. This area is cut longer than the green but shorter than the fairway.

ATTEND THE FLAG – To hold and remove the flagstick from the hole as your partner putts from a distance.

AWAY – (as in "you're away") A term that refers to a ball farthest from the hole, and thus the next to be played.

BACK NINE – The second half of an eighteen hole round of golf.

BACKSPIN – The backward rotation of the ball in flight, which creates lift, and upon landing reduces forward roll that can cause the ball to back up.

BACKSWING – The movement of taking a club back from the ball and up to the point at which the downswing begins with the intention of striking the ball.

BALL MARK – The indentation left by the ball when it lands on the green.

BALL MARKER – A small flat object, often a coin, used to mark or indicate the ball's position on the green.

BALL WASHER – A free standing device usually located near the tee box used to clean golf balls.

BIRDIE – A term for a score of one under par for a hole.

BITE – The action of a ball that stops quickly upon landing, caused by a high degree of backspin. Often you'll hear professional golfers shout out "bite", hoping their ball stops as soon as it hits the ground or green.

BOGEY – A score of one over par for a hole.

BREAK – The path of a ball rolling on a putting surface that is not flat.

BUNKER – A hazard filled with sand; also called a sand trap.

CASUAL WATER – Water or soggy ground that is not a permanent water hazard. A golfer can lift the ball from casual water and replay it from the nearest point of relief (i.e., better position) no closer to the hole.

CHIP – A short, low-flying shot that usually occurs near the green.

CHIP-IN – A chip that goes in the hole.

CLUBFACE – The hitting area of a clubhead, usually featuring horizontal grooves or scoring lines.

CLUBHEAD – The portion of the club that comes in contact with the ball.

CLUBHOUSE – The building that includes the pro shop, lockers and dining facilities.

CUP – The hole on the green where your golf ball is hit.

DEUCE – To get the ball into the cup in two strokes (known as "holing out").

DIMPLE – The indentations on the surface of a golf ball that help create lift.

DIVOT – A piece of sod removed from the ground by the club during the stroke.

DOGLEG – A hole whose fairway curves either left or right.

DOUBLE BOGEY – A score of two over par for a hole.

DOUBLE EAGLE – A score of three under par for a hole.

DOWNSWING – The part of the swing in which the clubhead is moving toward the ball.

DRAW – A golf shot that is made to curve slightly to the left – the opposite of a fade.

DRIVE – A shot played from a tee box.

DRIVER – The number 1 wood. The driver is the largest club and is used from the teeing ground for maximum distance.

DRIVING RANGE – The area where golf is taught and practiced.

DROP – The procedure by which you put an out-of-play ball back into play.

EAGLE – A score of two under par for a hole.

EMBEDDED BALL – When a portion or the entire ball remains in its pitch-mark, (where it landed) usually in soft ground. Also known as "plugged".

EXECUTIVE COURSE – A golf course, either 9 holes or 18 holes, which is shorter in length than a regulation course.

EXPLOSION SHOT – A full-swing shot played from a bunker in which the clubhead strikes the sand behind and underneath the ball, propelling the ball out of the bunker with the displaced sand.

FACE – The surface of the club designed for hitting the ball.

FADE – A ball that is meant to curve slightly to the right – the opposite of a draw.

FAIRWAY – An area of tended grass between the teeing ground and green on each hole.

FIRST CUT – The part of the rough, only a few yards wide, that lines the edge of the fairway. The grass on the rough is a little longer than the grass on the fairway.

FLAGSTICK – The pole with a flag that indicates the location of the hole on the putting green.

FLIGHT – The path the ball takes through the air.

FOLLOW-THROUGH – The part of the swing that occurs after the ball has been struck.

FORE – A word shouted to alert other golfers that an errant shot has been hit and a golf ball is headed in their direction.

FOURSOME – a group of four players.

FRONT NINE – The first half of an eighteen hole round of golf.

GIMME – A short putt that your partners concede because they don't expect you to miss it. A gimme counts as one stroke.

GREEN – The entire course over which the game is played, not just the area commonly called the putting green.

GREENS FEE – What a golfer pays to play a course.

GRIP – A term that refers to the rubber or leather handle of a golf club, and also how the club is held within the hands – your grip.

GROUNDING – To rest the flange of a club on the ground while preparing to hit the ball. Not permitted in a hazard.

GROUND UNDER REPAIR – An area of the golf course from which a player is entitled relief (free drop) without penalty. This area could be casual water, damaged turf, or an area under renovation.

HANDICAP – A term that refers to the number of strokes given to a player based on the average of scores turned in, allowing players of different ability the chance to compete with each other.

HANDICAP INDEX – A number that represents the potential ability of a player, derived from the handicap formula.

HAZARD – An area of the golf course, usually sand or water, from which no relief (see "relief" below) is allowed.

HEAD – The part of the club which strikes the ball.

HEEL - The part of the club that joins the shaft to the clubhead.

HOLE IN ONE – A hole played in one stroke. Also known as an Ace.

HOLE OUT – To take consecutive putts to finish a hole, regardless of other golfers' positions on the green. This is usually done to speed up play.

HONOR – The privilege of playing the first shot on a hole by having made the lowest score on the previous hole.

HOOK – A shot that curves from right to left, caused by an inside-out swing path – the opposite of a slice.

IN PLAY – The ball is considered "in play" as soon as a player takes a stroke from the teeing ground until the ball is holed out, lost, out-of-bounds, lifted from a hazard or another ball is substituted.

INSIDE THE LEATHER – A gimme putt that is no farther from the hole than the length of the grip end of a putter.

INTERLOCKING GRIP – A type of grip which the little finger of the left hand is entwined with the index finger of the right hand (for a right-handed player).

IRON – A type of club with a tilted metal blade for its head that hits the ball high in the air so it lands with little roll.

LAG – A long putt intended to come to a rest near the hole.

LATERAL HAZARD – A hazard, usually water, marked by red stakes.

LAY-UP – A shot played conservatively to avoid a hazard or difficult location.

LIE   Where the ball comes to rest.

LIFT AND CLEAN   Under certain conditions, a player may pick up the ball, clean off any attached mud, and then replace it without penalty.

LINE – The intended path of the ball.

LIP – The edge of the hole or bunker.

LOB SHOT – A shot with maximum height but minimum distance.

LOFT – The degree to which the clubface is angled backward, designed to lift the ball in the air. A club's loft determines how high and far your shot will travel.

LPGA – Ladies Professional Golf Association, founded in 1950.

MARSHAL – The golf course person responsible for keeping the pace of play moving to avoid slow play on the course.

MULLIGAN – A replayed shot, taken by a player dissatisfied with their first shot. (Not permitted in tournament golf.)

NET SCORE – Score for a hole or round after handicap strokes are deducted.

NINETY DEGREE RULE – A local ruling that asks cart riding players to cross fairways on a 90 degree angle, usually in effect during wet course conditions.

OUT OF BOUNDS – The area outside the golf course where a golfer cannot play their ball, usually marked by white stakes or white line.

OVERLAPPING – Describes a grip in which the little finger of the right hand lies over the index finger of the left hand (for right-handed players).

PAR – The standard score or error-free play. Par for a typical 18-hole course is 72 with ten holes being par-4's, four holes being par-5's and four holes being par-3's.

PENALTY STROKE – A stroke added to a player's score for a hole or a round under the penalty clauses in the Rules of Golf.

PGA – Professional Golfers' Association – the governing body of the U.S. Club Professionals, established in 1916.

PIN – Another word for flagstick which marks the location of the hole on the putting green.

PIN HIGH – A ball that comes to rest at a point level with the hole for distance, but not necessarily near the pin.

PITCH – A short, high approach shot onto the putting green.

PITCHING WEDGE – An iron club with a high-lofted clubface that is used to hit short, high approach shots to the green.

PLAYING THROUGH – When invited, the act of passing a golfer or group of golfers that are playing in front of you, usually because the player or group is not able to keep up with the pace of play.

PRACTICE SWING – Any swing taken by a player without the intention of striking the ball.

PRO SHOP – The part of the clubhouse where greens fees are paid and where equipment can be purchased.

PROVISIONAL – A second ball played in case the original ball is lost or out of bounds.

PUTT – A shot in which a player uses a putter to roll the ball across the green and toward the hole with the purpose of "holing out".

PUTTER – An almost straight-faced club designed to stroke the ball along the ground on the putting green.

QUADRUPLE BOGEY – A score of four over par for a hole.

RELIEF – Permission to drop the ball in a more desirable position with no penalty.

ROUGH – Ground on the course, usually flanking the fairway, where the grass is thicker and longer than elsewhere.

ROUND – Eighteen holes of golf played consecutively.

RUB OF THE GREEN – The name given for a bad bounce or unexpected movement to the golf ball caused by an outside source.

SAND TRAP – A bunker.

SAND WEDGE – A lofted iron club used for hitting the ball out of the sand.

SCORECARD – A card that lists the hole length, par and handicap rating of each hole, where the player marks down the total number of strokes taken on each hole.

SHAFT – The part of the club that joins the clubhead and grip end.

SHORT GAME – Shots played on or around the putting green.

SHOT – The result of striking the ball.

SIT – When the ball comes to a stop.

SLICE – A shot that curves from left to right for a right-handed player – opposite of a hook.

SLOPE RATING – The difficulty of a course used in handicap calculations. The higher the Slope Rating, the more difficult the course.

STANCE – The standing position of a golfer when addressing the ball.

STARTER – A course official who determines when play begins and from which teeing area.

STIFF – A term that describes a shaft which has very little flex. Also an expression used to describe a ball that is hit very close to the hole.

STROKE – An intended swing which counts whether or not the player contacted the ball.

SWING PLANE – The angle at which the club travels on a rounded arc around the body during the swing.

TAKEAWAY – The start of the backswing. The act of taking the club away from the ball to start the swing.

TAP-IN – A very short putt.

TEE – A wooden or plastic peg that the ball rests on to begin your tee shot. Also known as the area in which a player hits the ball to begin each hole.

TEE MARKERS – Two objects that define where the ball can be teed up. The ball can be placed anywhere within two club-lengths behind the markers.

TEE UP – To place the ball on a tee.

TEE TIME – The time a round begins as determined by the starter.

TIGHT – A course that is narrow with well guarded greens.

TOE – The part of the clubhead farthest from the shaft.

TOPPED – A short or low-trajectory shot created when the clubhead hits the top of the ball.

TOPSPIN – The forward rotation of the ball in flight. Topspin adds run to the ball.

TRAP – A sand bunker.

TRIPLE BOGEY – Three over par for a hole.

UNDER PAR – Taking fewer shots than par on a hole or for the round.

UNPLAYABLE LIE – A position of the ball that makes it difficult or impossible to play the next shot.

USGA – United States Golf Association, one of the game's two governing bodies.

WATER HAZARD – Any pond, lake, river or ditch on the course marked by yellow posts.

WEDGE – A metal club designed for loft, mostly used for high approach and sand shots.

WHIFF – To miss the ball during a swing, which counts as a stroke.

WINTER RULES – Local rules applied during the winter season which take into account inferior course conditions.

WOODS – Clubs used for long shots, usually off the tee or fairway.

YARDAGE MARKERS – Signs located along the fairway usually on sprinkler heads or small stone plates, showing the distance to the middle of the green from that spot to assist golfers with club selection.

Notes

Notes

Chapter 10

Employment Opportunities in Golf

EMPLOYMENT OPPORTUNITIES IN GOLF

Has your child expressed an interest in golf or in working at a golf course? A golf course is a great place to gain summer or part-time employment for youngsters. Besides providing the perfect environment to improve their game, golf course employment offers the opportunity to learn the values, camaraderie, etiquette and sportsmanlike qualities associated with the game of golf. It is also an excellent place to determine whether your child might be interested in pursuing a long-term career as a golf professional. Summer jobs for children offered at a golf course facility are golf club storage handlers, caddies (usually on private courses), collecting range balls, and course maintenance. Children can begin working at a golf course facility assisting on the driving range and other necessary tasks, as early as 8 years of age. Because of their young age, children are not usually paid any monetary remuneration for their work, but are allowed free access to the golf course during slower parts of the day. Children 16 years and older, who have a driver's permit, can assist with arranging golf carts for golfers and for tournaments, as well as working in the bag shop cleaning and arranging golf members' clubs, for which they are paid a salary.

As a post-secondary student, your son or daughter may wish to pursue a career in golf other than as a golf tour player. There are numerous golf career paths, and organizations like the PGA offers a Professional Readiness Orientation program. Some of the many careers offered in the golf field are:

HEAD GOLF PROFESSIONAL – owns and operates a golf shop or supervises the direction of the golf shop and supervision of teaching at the golf facility.

DIRECTOR OF GOLF – directs the total golf operation of a golf facility, including the golf shop, golf range, golf car operations (if applicable), and supervision of the Head Golf Professional.

TEACHING PROFESSIONAL – individuals employed at a golf facility or school as a golf instructor, supervisors of golf instructors or individuals who instruct professionals how to teach.

ASSISTANT GOLF PROFESSIONAL – an individual who is employed at a golf facility and spends at least 50% of the time working on club repair, merchandising, handicapping records, inventory control, bookkeeping and tournament operations.

OWNERSHIP AND LEASING/EXECUTIVE MANAGEMENT – individuals who are employed in professional positions in management, development, ownership, operation and/or financing of facilities.

GOLF CLINICIAN – an individual whose main source of income is golf shows or clinics.

COLLEGE GOLF COACH – individuals who are employed as golf coaches at accredited colleges, universities and junior colleges.

DIRECTOR OF INSTRUCTION – an individual who is managing, supervising and directing the total teaching program at a golf school or golf facility.

GOLF RETAIL – ownership or management of golf products or services at a golf retail facility.

GOLF CADDIE – an individual who carries a golfer's bag, gives insightful advice and moral support.

GOLF COURSE DEVELOPMENT – individuals who are employed in the design of golf courses as architects or who are employed in an ownership or management capacity as golf course builders.

BROADCASTING/JOURNALISM – individuals employed in the reporting, editing, writing or publishing of golf-related publications in any form of media, or in the broadcasting or commentating about golf events on network television, cable networks, the Internet or any other form of related media.

GOLF MANUFACTURER MANAGEMENT – individuals employed in an executive, administrative or supervisory position with a golf industry manufacturer or golf industry distributor.

SALES REPRESENTATIVE – individuals employed by one or more golf manufacturing or distributing companies involved in the wholesale sales and distribution of golf merchandise or golf-related supplies to golf facilities, retail stores or any other golf outlets.

TOURNAMENT DIRECTOR – individuals employed in the coordination, planning and implementation of golf events for organizations, businesses or associations.

RULES OFFICIAL – individuals employed in the provision of services as a rules official for recognized golf associations, golf tours or golf events.

GOLF EQUIPMENT SPECIALIST – individuals employed in the business of club fitting.

Notes

Notes

Chapter 11

Golf Associations & Federations
That can help Your Child
In their Golf Career

GOLF ASSOCIATIONS AND FEDERATIONS THAT CAN HELP YOUR CHILD IN THEIR GOLF CAREER

AMERICAN JUNIOR GOLF ASSOCIATION – is a nonprofit organization dedicated to the overall growth and development of young men and women who aspire to earn college golf scholarships through competitive junior golf.
www.ajga.org
(877)-373-2542 or (770) 868-4200

INTERNATIONAL JUNIOR GOLF TOUR – provides exceptional junior golfers with the opportunity to develop and showcase their competitive skills while setting high standards to preserve the traditions and integrity of the game. The IJGT features 70 golf tournaments in the United States as well as tournaments in Canada, Mexico, Colombia and Scotland.
www.ijgt.com
(843)-785-2444

LADIES PROFESSIONAL GOLF ASSOCIATION (LPGA) – impacts the lives of young women by providing learning facilities and educational programs that promote character development and life-enhancing values through the game of golf.
www.lpga.com
(386)-274-6200

NATIONAL MINORITY GOLF FOUNDATION – utilizes golf as a vehicle for educational opportunities through competitive junior golf in hopes of earning college golf scholarships for minority junior golfers.
www.nmgf.memfirstweb.net
(904)-940-4300

PARS JUNIOR GOLF FOUNDATION, INC. (Parental Assistance Referral Service) – this organization has helped students who wish to attend college and compete in collegiate golf. Athletic scholarships and financial aid are available for students that meet the minimum mandatory requirements of the NCAA, NAIA and Junior College levels.
www.parsjuniorgolf.com
(803) 641-1952

PROFESSIONAL GOLF ASSOCIATION OF AMERICA (PGA of AMERICA) – is the world's largest working sports organization comprised of 28,000 men and women golf professionals who are the recognized experts in growing, teaching and managing the game of golf. The PGA offers The Callaway Golf PGA Junior Series to boys and girls representing all 50 states and 22 countries. Many of the PGA Junior Series' top players have received partial to full golf scholarships to NCAA colleges and universities. The mission of the PGA Junior Series is to provide affordable and competitive playing opportunities for youths between 13 and 18 years old.
www.pga.com
(561)-624-8400

CANADIAN PROFESSIONAL GOLF ASSOCIATION – is a member-based, non-profit organization representing over 3500 golf professionals across Canada.
www.cpga.com
(800) 782-5764 or (519) 853-5450

ROYAL CANADIAN GOLF ASSOCIATION – is the governing body of golf in Canada. Their mission is to promote participation in and a passion for the game while protecting its traditions and integrity. The RCGA through the RCGA Foundation has committed substantial funds to Canadian university golf and believes in the importance of providing credible, reasonably priced, quality education to students interested in obtaining a Canadian educational golf scholarship.
www.rcga.org
(905)-845-7040

TIGER WOODS FOUNDATION – is an educational facility that takes young people beyond the classroom and challenges them to change their world. The TWF offers grants awarded to education and youth development programs across the country on a quarterly basis. The Tiger Woods Foundation also founded the Tiger Woods Foundation National Junior Golf Team for underserved youth to help those children not historically given the opportunity to excel in golf.
www.tigerwoodsfoundation.org
(949)-725-3003

UNITED STATES GOLF ASSOCIATION – is a centralized body that writes the rules, conducts national championships and establishes a national system of handicapping. Each year, the USGA conducts 13 national championships, 10 of which are strictly for amateurs. They offer grants to help organizations develop introductory golf programs and alternative golf facilities for youth from disadvantaged backgrounds, minority youth, girls and individuals with disabilities.
www.usga.org
(800)-223-0041 or (908) 234-2300

YOUNG GOLFERS OF AMERICA ASSOCIATION – develops, maintains and coordinates programs that encourages youth to participate in golf while enhancing a greater sense of integrity, imagination and honesty.
www.ygaa.org
(323)-292-7030

Notes

Notes

Chapter 12

Golf Schools, Camps & Academies

GOLF SCHOOLS, CAMPS AND ACADEMIES

The following is a list of some of the main golf camps, programs and schools offered throughout the United States and Canada. Most local golf courses also offer daily, weekly, private or semi-private golf instruction.

DAVID LEADBETTER GOLF ACADEMY – offers short term golf programs, full time golf programs, tour preparation programs and post-graduate golf programs.
www.davidleadbetter.com
(888) 633-5323 or (407) 787-3330

THE FIRST TEE – provides a learning facility and educational programs that promote character development and life-enhancing values through the game of golf. They provide affordable access to golf especially for kids who might not otherwise have an opportunity to play the game.
www.thefirsttee.org
(904) 940-4300

INTERNATIONAL JUNIOR GOLF ACADEMY – offers weekly summer golf camps, full-time boarding programs for kids from grades 6 to high school graduates. The IJGA prepares junior golfers for success in academics and tournament golf and assists students in finding appropriate colleges and universities where they can play golf competitively.
www.ijga.com
(843) 686-1500

LADIES PROFESSIONAL GOLF ASSOCIATION – The LPGA–USGA Girls Golf was formed to provide golf programs for girls from the ages of 7 to 17 to learn to play golf, build lasting friendships and experience competition in a fun, supportive environment, preparing them for a lifetime of enjoyment with the game.
www.lpga.com
(386) 274-6200

PGA TOUR GOLF ACADEMY – offers weekly junior golf camp programs.
www.pga.com
(800) 766-7939

U.S. KIDS GOLF – offers kids ages 6 to 12, along with their parents, to a fun and challenging three-day golf camp.
www.uskidsgolf.com
(888)-387-5437

BRENT MORRISON GOLF ACADEMY (CANADA) – offers golf summer camps for beginners, intermediate and advanced players, as well as post-secondary tour preparation.
www.brentmorrisongolf.com
(877) 407-4653 or (250) 752-8786

JUNIOR GOLF ACADEMY OF CANADA – located in Florida, the JGAC offers yearly golf instruction and secondary school academics. They also offer summer golf programs in northern Ontario.
www.jgac.ca
(416) 688-0641

RANDLE GOLF (CANADA) – offers golf programs from junior camps to year long programs for juniors, to golf university for graduate and post-graduate students.
www.randlcgolf.com
(250) 818-6666

Notes

Chapter 13

Children-Friendly Golf Holidays & Resorts

CHILDREN-FRIENDLY GOLF HOLIDAYS AND RESORTS

There's no better way to spend time with your children or grandchildren, than taking them on a family golfing holiday. Golf is one of the only sports that encourages family togetherness – both males and females. Golf resorts are recognizing the popularity of the family-oriented golf holiday, and they are cooperating by placing junior tees or tee markers on their courses, and making the layout a shorter distance for junior golfers. Many golf resorts are offering reduced greens fees for children, and some are offering free greens fees to children aged 15 and under after 3:00 p.m., along with free club rentals and free lessons, provided they are there with a paying adult.

Here are a number of children-friendly golf resorts you may want to investigate for your next family golf holiday, but also check with resort.com, golf.worldsbestdeals.com, and golfaldo.com for other options. Note also that rates, fees, etc. are subject to change. All Web site addresses and telephone numbers for resorts, golf associations and academies were accurate at the time of this printing, but such information changes frequently.

PINEHURST RESORT
Pinehurst, NC
www.pinehurst.com
(800) 487-4653 or (910) 295-6811
Free lodging, food and greens fees for children 12 and under, with a paying adult.

KIAWAH ISLAND GOLF RESORT
Kiawah Island, SC
www.kiawahresort.com
(800) 654-2924 or (843) 768-2121
In the summer months, children 17 and under enjoy free greens fees with a paying adult, from 6:30 to 7:00 p.m.

HERSHEY RESORT
Hershey, PA
www.hersheypa.com
(800) 437-7439
The nine-hole Spring Creek Golf Course for kids is only $12.00 on weekends. The 2079-yard par 33 course is ideal for junior golfers. They also offer instruction, club fitting and summer golf competition.

CELEBRATION
Celebration, FL
www.celebrationgolf.com
(407) 566-4653 or (888) 275-2918
The junior course is $1.00. Adults must be accompanied by a paying child! The Celebration Golf Course's 18-hole course has permanent junior tee boxes at 2,220 yards.

PALMETTO DUNES RESORT
Hilton Head Island, SC
www.palmettodunes.com
(866) 292-4148
The Family get-away package includes villa accommodations, two days unlimited golf, $25.00 gift card, bike rental, one hour of tennis and a golf clinic, starting at $149.00 per person, per night for a family of four.

HYATT REGENCY SCOTTSDALE RESORT AND SPA AT GAINEY RANCH
Scottsdale, AZ
www.scottsdale.hyatt.com
(480) 444-1234
Children play for free June 13 to September 4 and for $25.00 with a paying adult thereafter. They offer *junior tees*, special tee locations designed to provide children 12 and under with an opportunity to play a "yardage-friendly" round of golf on a par 72 course.

GRAND TRAVERSE RESORT AND SPA
Acme, MI
www.grandtraverseresort.com
(800) 236-1577
Spruce run has junior tee markers. On The Bear and The Wolverine courses, kids can tee off from the fairway. The Grand Family Escape Package includes accommodation, arcade tokens, in-room movie or video game, and ice cream for four, starting at $183.00 per person per night in the summer months – less in the fall season.

WILD DUNES RESORT
Isle of Palms, SC
www.wilddunes.com
(888) 778-1876
The Family and Evening Golf program allows children 15 and under to play free with a paying adult after 5:00 p.m. Their golf package for juniors is $65.00 to play the Links course and $40.00 for the Harbor course any time after 11:00 a.m. any day of the week.

WINTERGREEN RESORT
Wintergreen, VA
www.wintergreenresort.com
(800) 926-3723
The midweek Champions Challenge includes lodging in a two-bedroom condo, unlimited golf, range balls, a $25.00 Callaway Golf merchandise certificate and access to the Aquatics and Fitness Center for $150.00 per person, double occupancy.

THE WIGWAM GOLF RESORT AND SPA
Litchfield Park, AZ
www.wigwamresort.com
(866) 716-8136
The Timeless Golf Package includes one night's stay, unlimited golf at all three courses for parents, cart, bag storage and use of practice facilities starting at $139.00 per person in the summer; $299.00 in the Fall/$409.00 double occupancy. None of the three 18-hole layouts have junior tees, but Little Wigwam Golf Links is a three-hole course where parents and children can play together.

THE WESTIN KIERLAND RESORT AND SPA
Phoenix, AZ
www.kierlandresort.com
(800) 354-5892
The Kierland Golf Club offers junior golf fees. Children playing golf with their parents pay half the price of the greens fees. Junior golf club rentals are available, and junior tees are offered on the Mesquite course – one of Kierland's three nine-hole courses. This family-friendly golf club holds several golf clinics throughout the year geared toward children 8–15 years of age. The four-day clinic includes 3 hours of instruction each day.

SKAMANIA LODGE
Stevenson, WA
www.skamania.com
(509) 427-7700
After 5:00 p.m., Sunday and Tuesday evenings, enjoy a modified course set-up on the back 9 holes, complete with Earl's footsteps as markers (Skamania Lodge's Bigfoot mascot) for the family to tee off from, providing achievable distances. Family golf price is $25.00 for parents, including car and free for children 18 and under if accompanied by a parent. Rentals provided at no charge for children; $5.00 for adults.

Notes

Some Final Words on Golf

SOME FINAL WORDS ON GOLF

Congratulations on introducing your son or daughter to the wonderful world of golf. As a parent, you can greatly influence your child's desire to play golf by serving as an excellent role model. Children pattern themselves after their parents and mentors, and if your own behavior on the driving range or on the golf course is positive and upbeat, your child will continue to enjoy themselves as well. Golf is a sport that enables families of all ages and all abilities to get involved and have fun together. It's a sport that can be enjoyed for a lifetime. The benefit and enrichment of friendships, family bonding, and business interactions can all be attained through this fascinating sport. So have fun from tee to green and everything in between.

From Tee to Green for Tot to Teen: A Parent's Guide to Getting Your Child Started in Golf is distributed by **the booklegger.**

There are three ways to order copies of this book:

- Telephone Orders: (800) 262-1556
- Fax Orders: (800) 250-2199
- Through the Internet: See below

Retailers
visit *the booklegger at:*
www.booklegger.com

Consumers
visit *GolfSmart at:*
www.golfsmart.com

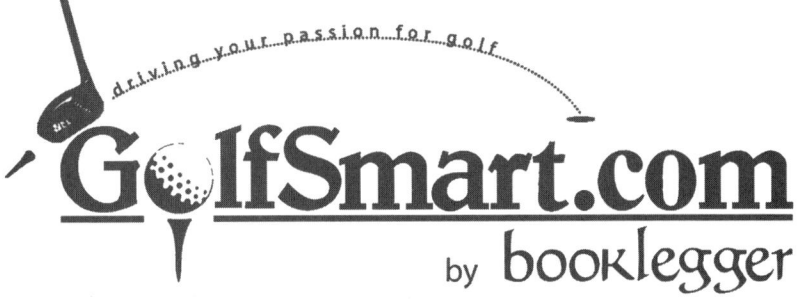